As You Slip Away

A poetry book on grief and healing

Aniqah Be

As You Slip Away

Edition 1
ISBN: 978-976-96840-1-0

Written and illustrated by Aniqah Be
Edited by Amaara Beharry

Aniqah Be

Aniqah Be is an Indo-Caribbean, Muslim creative and archer from Trinidad and Tobago. She pours her heart, mind & soul into her words, and her blood, sweat, tears, prayers & fears into her art. Aniqah is a woman of many hats and enjoys continuous learning. She believes in striving to be a better you than you were yesterday.

Find more of her work here:
@aniqahbe - Instagram, Facebook, LinkedIn
aniqahbe.carrd.co

For those of us who remain behind,
To hold onto the love and grief

And to those who have left us,
And moved on,
We will always love you

Foreword

Writing is like breathing to me, and this cathartic nature is emphasized throughout this book. This book was written over the course of a few days, as I franticly needed an outlet to process my grief and sorrow.

This book was unplanned. It came to me in a moment and my fingers moved desperately to get all the words down. I had so many plans for all the books I ever wanted to release; this book desecrated my plans and demanded to be written and read.

I want to thank my parents for their strength, and my grandparents and my family for all the love they shower me with. Thank you to Aunty Vernie and Aunty Avisha for inspiring me with the prompt that lead to this explosion of poetry. And finally, thank you to my rock, my sister, the truest of unconditional loves, for being the first and only person I trust to read and edit my poetry. Weeks after our loss, you sat with this book and made it ours. I love you all more than you will ever know.

This cover is so special to me. It incorporates the favourite flowers of my grandparents.

- ❖ *Pink roses for Mama Afrose*
- ❖ *Orchids for Mama Shanti*
- ❖ *Bougainvillea for Papa Irvin*
- ❖ *Hibiscus and lotus for Papa Muntaz (if you know, you know)*

Acknowledgement

Amaara, my best friend, my sister,
Thank you for believing in me and my dreams,
Thank you for being my constant strength.

My parents, my rocks,
Thank you for encouraging me to brave strange seas,
And for spoiling me with your love to no end.

And to my grandparents:
Mama Afrose, The Keeper of Peace,
Thank you for showing me the power of love and resilience.
Papa Muntaz, The Provider,
Thank you for teaching the beauty of unconditional love.

Mama Shanti, The Stitcher,
Thank you for reminding me that what I sew, I shall reap.
Papa Irvin, The Watchman,
Thank you for emphasizing the value of our fleeting time.

Aunty Zorie, The Lover,
Thank you for cementing that I was never alone so I always knew someone out there loved me.
Uncle Wazeer, The Heart,
Thank you for taking care of me when it was hard to see a time where I could breathe easily.

Table of Contents

Part I
Before You Go

You Wanted To Go

You told me you wanted to go,
And I held my breath like I held my tongue.
No words could come to my writer's mouth,
Nothing of reasoning besides "No, you cannot."
How could you be ready,
When there is no way I could ever have been?
How could you say those words so calmly,
While I just sat there staring?
I sat, bewildered, confused, and shocked,
And couldn't fathom how someone so loved
Would want to go,
And all I could think of, was pleading,
"I love you. Please don't leave me. Don't. Please."

If I Ignore The Signs

In the beginning, there's a sense of Normal,
Until there isn't anymore.

We see the signs, as you shrink into a smaller semblance
of yourself,
And deem it "growing pains", pack it into an old box to
place on the shelf,
Call it Normal, and move on.

They say to ignore crying babies so they'll learn to stop
on their own,
So whenever you spoke of when it would be time to
go,
We would laugh it off and retreat into the comfort of
our televisions and phones,
Pretending your warnings and comments were ordinary
odes to your life,
Just wanting to believe that EVERYTHING WILL BE
FINE.

"... deem it "growing pains"

pack it into an old box to place on
the shelf,

Call it Normal, and move on"

Just Keep Trying

I know you want to leave,
But please just can't you try
I don't want you to go,
I don't want you to die.
I don't want you to leave this world,
And leave me here alone behind.
I need you to continue on,
I need you to fight.

I'll do everything I can on my end.
I'll feed you all the love you need
I promise not to move from your side,
If you say that you won't leave.

Just keep trying,
Don't give up,
Don't go,
Just keep pushing on,
I know that you are hurting,
But please,
Continue to be strong.

As you get smaller and weaker,
I continue to plead,
And beg and hope and pray,
I just need you here with me,
I just want you to stay.

I know it's hard,
I don't know how *hard* it is,

But I cannot fathom a world,
With you not in it.

I am angry with our souls
That eventually leaves our bodies
I am angry with our bodies
For being so fickle and weak
I am angry with Time
For it's tick-tick-tick-ing on
I am angry with the world
For not doing more.

I am angry with you, but not really,
Though it may seem so,
But it's just my love, dressed differently,
Because I so desperately, am begging,
Please don't go.

I don't want to have to let you go.

"I'll feed you all the love you need"

There is Nothing I Can Do

Watching you slip is away,
Is an especially painful thing
When I feel like I can see your pain
But all I can do... is nothing.

I watch you fake smiles for me,
To pretend it's all okay,
All you want is my peace of mind,
But all I want and won't have is for you to stay.

Your smiles get harder as time ticks on,
Even as I make all those little jokes you'd once enjoyed,
Do you remember every moment we shared?
Because I'm desperately trying to write them all down.

I know that one day we'll all move on,
And in years to come, we'll all return to the earth and
her flowers,
But I don't want to even think of a world,
In which we are not here together.

"Do you remember every moment
we shared?

Because I'm desperately trying to
write them all down."

You Are Going Home

You are going away for a while,
That's what I am trying to tell myself,
You're going somewhere better than here,
To a place where you will have
No worry, no pain, no anxiety, and no fear.
You will be okay when you go,
And so too, will I... I think.
The world will keep spinning,
And time will keep turning.
One day we'll be reunited,
That's what I HAVE to believe,
Because it's what I need
To let you know it's okay for you to move on,
So you don't have to worry about me.

Time To Say Goodbye

"Time to go home"
Is almost always met with tears and whining,
"Please let us stay just for a while longer"
Pleading to play with our friends and partners in crime,
Rarely would our luck strike, instead being scooped into
our parents' arms

"Time to head home"
We would regrettably tell our pals at parties and bars,
Relieved to soon curl up in the warmth of our covers
When we have had our fun and are spent for the night

"Time to return home"
Is what they say sometimes before they leave
To head into that eternal light,
Where a home is quite more than a roof over your
head
But God's loving embrace and mercy instead

"Time to go home"
Is harder when the home doesn't seem as complete
When it's no longer the "we" that it used to be,
And I keep looking around for the You
That helped to make me, "me"

""Time to return home"

Is what they say sometimes before
they leave

To head into that eternal light,..."

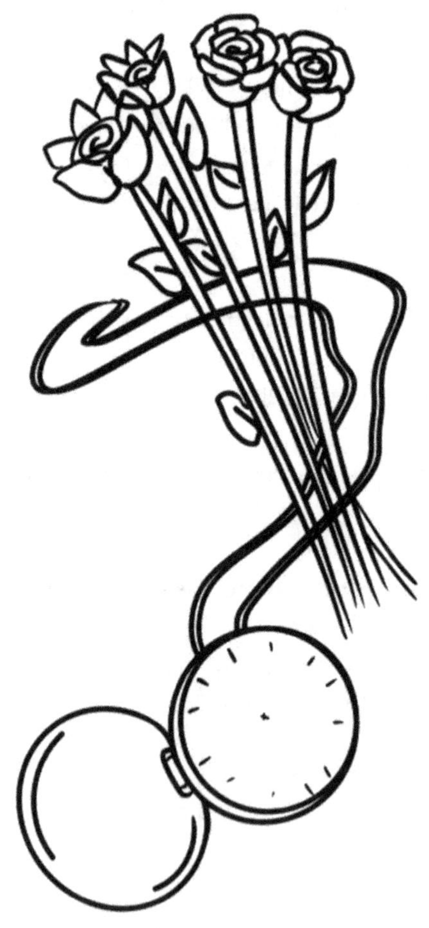

Part II
After They Leave

When The News Comes

In the moment there's a pause in time,
When your breath hitches - neither inhaled nor exhaled,
Just floating in the space between Time and Fate,
Along with the confirmation that you have gone.

Sometimes it hits like the first raindrop on your skin on
a gloomy day
Or the sudden crack of thunder after lightning warns the
sky.
Occasionally it comes earth-shattering, rocking the earth,
The ground slipping from under, no way to predict the
quake.

Either way, the sound of your own heartbeat is a tremor
to the soul,
Holding your breath, not knowing what world you're in
anymore,
The shock electrifying any ordinary reflexes you might
have had,
For those, were normal in a different place, where your
loved one once was.

It Isn't Real

If I think about it too hard,
Then I will feel it, and I don't want to.
If I pretend it isn't real,
All I have to do is tell a half-truth,
That I miss you
But I'll see you again soon.

When I walk past the memories in time,
Where you have once been,
I think of it fondly,
And then promptly bury it deep in my mind again,
It was once so but now, it is not
Just hide it away in the crevices of my heart.

When I think of something I have to tell you,
And momentarily forget you're not here anymore,
I write it down somewhere and wallow,
And then pretend that nothing happened
And send messages to your old number...
Until it's no longer yours.

I cannot believe that you are no longer here,
When you were here just then and were so *you*
And now I look around for you,
In all the things you used to do,
But though I find you, in the littlest of things that are
still here,
It's not the *you* that you were; it could never compare.

16

Why Aren't You Here?

I had plans, and I know God is the Best of Planners,
But I had it all mapped out.
I had so many things I wanted to do with you,
That I'll never get to do now.
I have all the bucket lists and scraps of dreams left
behind,
I have all the memories you gifted me,
Painted all across my mind.
I have so many things that happen
Each and every day,
From the annoying anecdotes to the silly and the
mundane,
I don't know if you can see me
Or if you'll ever know
I don't know if you'll ever
Get to read all the words I will pen
And the un-freed books I wrote.
Were there things you never told me?
How will I ever know now?
I know you want me to have peace,
But how could you expect me not to spiral
Without you around?

I wish you didn't have to go,
I'm so angry at the world.
I wish that I could be with the ones I love always,
And I hope that will be so when I one day leave this
place.

"I have all the bucket lists and
scraps of dreams left behind,

I have all the memories you gifted
me,

Painted all across my mind."

If we had a little more time,
What could we have done with it?
Would we have soared through our bucket lists,
Or would we have (as we know) likely procrastinated?
Would you have told me all the things
That I desperately wish to know?
Would you have shared your innermost secrets?
Did you have more to grow?

If we had a little more time,
Would we have wasted it on movies and silly games?
Would we have filled our days with bacchanal and
drama,
Or would we have been brave enough to stand up on
every stage?
Would we have written all the stories that we ever
wanted to tell,
Would we have grabbed the pen of our own book and
take charge of as well?

If we grabbed the pen writing our lives,
Could we have scratched off what was ordained?
Is there another universe where you are not gone,
How can I get there?
Is there a way you could have been saved,
Was there any other way?
It's foolish to think, I know, that we could have changed
Fate,
But I long to dream of a world, wherein you got to
stay.

"But I long to dream of a world,
wherein you got to stay."

Not Anymore

Whenever I see those pesky flowers,
I think of you and how they made you smile,
And my heart breaks a little,
At how they too, will one day die.

Whenever I hear your name,
My heart pangs, like a doorbell was rang,
For I have stolen your soul and hidden it in my heart
I just hope no one can tell.

I give soft smiles and pretend I'm okay,
That I am just coping differently,
I see their attempts at subtle glances,
And I feel their anxiety when they worry.

I hoard my collections of photos and notes,
And videos from when you were bubbly and bright,
I wonder if pieces of your soul
Are within the comforting colours of those digital eyes

I yearn for the warmth of your hand,
And the wholeness of your loving embrace,
I long to return to the days of our best memories,
And pretend this was all just a dream.

I know it could never happen,
So I don't pray for it,
But I wish for it so desperately,
That you could be here still, with me.

"Whenever I see those pesky flowers,

I think of you and how they made
you smile"

What Do I Do Now?

It is said that everyone copes in their own way,
And I surely have seen that throughout my life.
But I don't know what to do,
I don't know how to be alright.

I tried everything, I tried keeping busy,
I buried myself in finding photos and writing eulogies,
I took short showers so I wouldn't think, and I
ferociously cleaned.
I drowned myself in work so I wouldn't have to feel.

I tried everything, I tried distractions,
I found movies and stories and games, but not for fun,
All I wanted was to keep my mind occupied and numb,
So it wouldn't have time to settle on the grief for too
long.

I tried everything, I tried talking, to those who know of
loss,
But our shared tears, do nothing but provoke my bitter
heart.
I tried to talk about you, but the words just can't come
out,
I can't think of what to say when you're no longer
around.

I tried everything, I tried to draw and write
To pour the pain of loss into something tangible and
real
To make the heavy plight of mourning somewhat lighter,

But I see no end to this abyss of sorrow anywhere in sight, it seems to stretch even wider.

You're Gone

You are gone now,
And though it hurts me, so deeply,
I have accepted
That you will not return to this earth.

I rest *somewhat* assured
That we will be reunited in Heaven,
Where we won't have a care in the world.
I know that your earthly pain is no more,
And God is surely the best of planners.
I appreciate the scarce time we were gifted,
And I will cherish our memories forever.
I will love you till the end of my time and even after,
I will pray to God for your love and peace in the
hereafter.

You are gone now,
But one day, I will leave this world too.
I know time heals all wounds,
But your loss will be a blow to my heart forever.
And yet, one day I will, God-willing, be reunited with
you
And all our loved ones, in Jannah.

26

Part III
Different

Cycles

As you slip away,
We cycle through the stages of grief,
Wishing and praying for you to be okay,
But knowing you will have to leave.

When you inevitably go,
The Heavens will celebrate your return,
To God, and to your forever Home,
While we remain here to mourn.

Some days the skies will cry with us,
Weeping "I miss you" so much,
On others, it will be as acrylic as our life,
And your gargantuan impact on others.

The sun will continue shining bright,
And the earth will revolve around the sun as it does,
The moon will pass by with playful winks,
But nothing will be just the same as it once was.

*"And the earth will revolve around
the sun as it does, ...*

*But nothing will be just the same as
it once was."*

Could Have Been

I think of the could have been's
Way too often,
All the dreams and stories and words,
All the things I never got to know.

I think of where you would've been
If you were still here,
And what you could and would have done.
I wonder if there was anything you'd want
For me to do - dreams you passed on,
Hidden in my grief of losing you.

I think of you fondly,
And I wish you could still be here,
I think of how you left,
And what I would bargain for *even just a few more*
years.

I think of how we use our time,
And what would be my could have been's
And so I try to live each day,
In memory of you, and how you'd want me to live.

"And what I would bargain for
even just a few more years."

BE
NEVER
COULD
IT
TIME
EVEN
IF
WE
COULD
HAVE
MORE
enough

Over My Grief

Excuse me, if you don't mind,
This grief here- it is mine.
I would rather not compare pumpkin vines with roots and
trees,
But your intensity is spilling resentment into my grief.

I am trying to control how much I pour into my cup
So it doesn't overrun and spill everywhere,
But you slosh your sorrow all over my mourning,
So I have to bottle it back and shove it deep in the
cupboard.

I see so many faces that I don't recognize.
I kissed all the cheeks and replied to the "How are you"
every time with soft smiles.
I know it should ease my heart how much you were
loved,
But I cannot help but feel annoyed when they cry
louder than us.

*"I am trying to control how much I
pour into my cup*

*So it doesn't overrun and spill
everywhere"*

Words of these Times

I don't have a talking stage in me right now,
Not when I can't get the wretched taste of emptiness
out of my mouth.
You speak of time like it's what I barter to you for our
friendship,
When I would have sullied different paths if it meant I
could buy a handful of moments more.

When I say I don't have the words,
I mean I can spill them through soulful tears over worn
handkerchiefs,
But the words won't dare escape my mouth
Not without my throat closing for fear my heart would
jump out.

When I tell you "not right now"
But you see me floating around in some other worldly
escape
Of pretentious books and cruel games
Who are you to judge... when you could just look
away?

What you don't understand about grief
Is that it's a gift, from my loved one, for me.
It is mine, and mine alone, like you have yours, and
they have theirs,
Each of our souls are different, in how we choose to
bear it.

So when I say "I need time", I will not bargain the
Heavens for more
But I will sit cuddling what is left of my loved one -
This grief - holding it tight, close to my heart,
With all my love, now and forevermore

I Am Sorry

I am sorry,
I cannot talk right now,
My grandpa just died
And only empty words would come from my mouth.

I am sorry,
I cannot console you on your slight inconvenience right
now
It's hard to hear anything through my tumultuous
breakdown

I am sorry for making everything all about me,
But my grief consumes everything I feel

I am sorry
For needing to retreat into myself,
To mend the shattered pieces of my soul,
Before I can reach out to anyone again

The silence echoes too loudly in my ears,
It's not you, or maybe it is,
I am trying to navigate this grief
I am sorry for the inconvenience of my sorrow

I am sorry.

- By Aniqah Be and Amaara Beharry

"It's hard to hear anything through
my tumultuous breakdown"

Never The Same

Every day I realize again and again,
That nothing will ever be the same

Memories of Savannah Grass days
With white wonders in the vast Cerulean Blue skies.
Nowadays the brightness just seem apathetically cruel,
When it's not a gloomy grey.

Even the sun shining
On everything and everyone,
Once in her Isoindoline Yellow — so bright,
Now we are all left covered by the shade of grief,
And nothing seems right.

Everyone feels the presence
Of the empty chair in every room,
And the teacup hiding in the kitchen,
Behind the enamel cups, in the early afternoon.

My mum misses her mum,
My dad misses his dad,
And I miss the way they were,
Before they were this sad
When I know there's nothing I could do
To ever bring them back.

I see the sadness in their eyes,
And I know it'll never be the same.
There is no way to take away their sorrow,

Not even if I brightened their skies with all the world's
acrylic paints.

Nothing will ever be the same,
Not mummy nor daddy, much less me
And none of us are okay,
This grief has changed us indefinitely.

The Tears Won't Fall

Your cries solidify my pain into cement,
That I use to fortify my walls.
You will not get in,
The Tears won't fall.

The massive blow from the cannons of Fate
Will only weaken my cracks but the wall will not break.
My resolution is impenetrable,
No matter the gravity of the heartache.

Alongside my crushed footmen and soldiers,
My resolve will be strengthened; it will never falter.
I will give my blood for my cause,
Come Hell or High Water.

In the darkest, loneliest, quietest corner walls,
I try to cry but cannot find the wherewithal,
After letting all others mourn, my tears have gone;
And now, the tears won't fall.

"Your cries solidify my pain into

cement,

That I use to fortify my walls.

You will not get in,

The Tears won't fall.

When The Funeral Flowers Wilt

Supposedly at some point,
I'll be called by the Fates
To the next stage, in the Cycle of Grief.
I wait with bated breath
Behind the velvet crimson curtains called Denial,
Words holding onto the cold air in my lungs
Holding on to one another for dear life...
Not wanting to be exhaled,
Despite in my throat, slowly dying.
Pungent roses rest upon their grave,
I can feel the bitterness of their decomposition -
Patience turns to terse nonchalance.

Shattered memories to sharp pieces of glass
Piercing my already-broken heart.
They all promise - it comes in waves,
That will eventually dull the edges.

What once was pain,
Will become beautiful crystal pieces of glass,
Sparkling on the shore, with the sand and stones and
shells,
Picked up by some passing artisan
Who'll turn it into something beautiful -
A bead of sweat and tears, from blood gone too soon,
No matter the borrowed time - it's always too soon.

And I'll wear it around my neck,
As a reminder of what once was -
So close to where the words were,

But now lay buried forevermore,
From my mind and my heart, they lived a lifetime
Waiting right behind my closed lips, to be said,
But could never be delivered to The Dead.

I keep seeing you in the steps you would take,
And our favourite enamel cup,
Everything reminds me of you -
And the way you would always keep your head up.

January is gone now - is it with you?
So too, are the flowers (there were so many,
You would have loved them)

We kept one of the dried roses - your last one,
I would like to believe that somewhere,
You're wearing it proudly in your hair.
The funerals flowers have wilted,
And one day, they too were gone,
Empty vases back under the sink,
Where they belong...

Until a neighbour brings yet another
Bouquet of Condolences and Love.
But when the moon passes for the 40th time
And the last of your flowers wilt,
I know that then, nothing will ever be the same,
For you will always be missed.

Died

When you died,
I held on to every part of you still here,
I smelled your sweet perfume,
Hidden in the corner of your room
When you used to brush my hair.
I hugged your old clothes and handkerchiefs,
I snuggled under the familiar warmth and comfort of
your blankets,
When it was dark, and I was scared.
I engraved all the pictures and videos in my mind,
Until one day, when I least expected it,
My phone shattered and died.
I tried everything I could,
I cried, knowing so much was now lost.
But I think this happened for a reason,
To remind me to live in the present,
And that you are not gone,
You are in my heart,
And everything else material could never last
As long as my love for you.
At the end of the day,
Control what you can
Everything else is confetti
That you'll deal with after the party.
One day these memories will be irrelevant,
When I am with you again,
And we'll have forever together to spend.

"I smelled your sweet perfume,

Hidden in the corner of your room

When you used to brush my hair."

In Your Own Words

Oh beautiful poet,
How I miss your penned words,
I search for them in memories,
And old messages where you shared your work!

Oh sweet genius,
How I miss your riddles and logic,
And how proud you would be of me,
For solving them, when others couldn't!

Oh gentle soul,
How I miss our conversations,
Where you shared your dreams and plans...
When I didn't know it would come to an end!

Oh beautiful poet,
How I despise you for crafting me a lie,
A glorious, rich poem, shown just to me,
Where you said you no longer wished to die!

Oh sweet genius,
How angry I am at you for leaving me behind,
With all these cryptic messages to analyze
Hoping and yearning for some possible explanation to
find!

Oh gentle soul,
How I wish you had confided in me your sorrow!
How I wish you told me you wanted to go!

How I wish I could have done something, if you had just
told me so!   49

Oh dearest friend,
How I resent you for the time you are away!
I will hug you when I, one day, see you again
When I finally get to tell you that I missed you, and "I
love you" again.

Falastin

Grief is worst when you are mourning
The loss of everything you have ever known —
Your loved ones, your home, your people, your roots,
Everything you believed to be true.

As sinners launch stones at your bleeding and bruised
exposed limbs,
And you stand before them pleading for empathy and
justice,
But they seek to take your everything —
Your voice, your land, your tents, your family, your
breath.

Every day that passes, we march on with our lives,
While you hide with what is left of those you love, to
deaf ears, we scream and plead and cry.

"Live to tell my story"[1], Refaat made us promise if he
returned to God,
And now that he is gone, there has been no less
bloodshed.
Numbers and statistics paint the gruesome truth of our
tainted world,
Now banned by The Corrupt, The Unconscionable and
The Evil.

---

[1] Refaat Alareer (23rd September 1979 — 6th December
2023) was a Palestinian poet, writer, professor, activist, Editor
of anthology "Gaza Writes Back", and martyr.

Fellow brothers and sisters lie under the same sun,
Contemplating their fate but never their faith.
While our leaders across the world debate equivocations,
Communities are levelled, children and innocent people
are massacred.

The young and brave take to the streets to protest for
justice,
While universities punish their students for speaking out
and encampments.
Screams and pleas worldwide for peace fall upon deaf
ears of elected leaders,
As parents in Gaza search for pieces of their children.

Damp land, tainted with the blood of the innocent, is
auctioned off.
Piers are built under the pretence of aid that will never
come.
Paper passes across blood-stained hands, heavy pockets
and tricky sleeves.
The world can only witness the origami news presented
on gory platters with gold spoons.

Across the digital world, posts pleading for help and to
be seen
Disappear into the ether of an algorithm with the bribed
heart of an artificial machine.
Bisan and others who post every day to remind us they
are alive,
Are isolated across oceans, to bide their time while the
world debates logic, emotion and empathy with lies.

Hiba warned us, "No poetry could ever bring it back:
what the lonely one has lost"[2]
When those who turned their gaze look at what their
greed has cost,
May they remember the Palestinians who sought solace
in prayer in the dark, dead nights,
When the "glow of the rockets"[3] provided sombre light.

Registries and youth will save and share the names of all
of those taken too soon,
Gone but never forgotten — we will never forget what
you chose to do
And we youth will ensure that History will forever
remember you throughout time
For the monsters that you are.

Free Palestine.

---

[2] Hiba Abu Nada (24th June 1991 – 20th October 2023)
was a Palestinian novelist, poet, acclaimed author of
"Oxygen is Not for the Dead", educator, nutritionist and
martyr.
[3] From one of Hiba's last public posts

Into That Good Night

May we go gently into that good night,
May we toil while we can, to reap what we sew
When it is our time to go.

We all must leave inevitably,
One day we will be but of the earth and dust,
When it is our time to go, we must.

May we go gently into that good night.
When our time comes, it will be alright,
However we go, we shall enter that eternal light.

Gently into that good night, may we go,
May we use our time to enrichen our lives,
So when we go, we are full of the brightest light.

May we go gently into that good night,
Amidst the prayers and crying of the loves of our lives,
When it is our time to go, may it all be alright.

Hush, Don't Cry For Me

When you told me not to cry for you,
I couldn't understand.
Surely you'd know I would be devastated
If you were no longer there to hold my hand.
You must know how I would be distraught,
If you were no longer there,
To shower me with your unconditional love.
How could you expect me not to cry,
When my earth would be shattered
Beyond recognition?

I did not understand it then,
But now I think I do,
You wanted me to be strong,
Not just for me, but for you.

So to my loved ones, when I go,
Do not cry for me too much,
Know that I have lived the life I was promised by God,
And I know how much I was loved.
Do not be sad, when I go or where or how or why,
I don't tell you not cry,
But don't let the grief consume your life.

Know that I lived as I did,
For us all and God to bear witness,
And know that if I am there with Him,
I am in a better place,
So please, just pray for my forgiveness.
Ask God to forgive me for all my bad deeds,

And pray to God that we shall find each other in the
hereafter,
To embrace one day again,
When all we shall feel is love, no longer as grief.

"So to my loved ones, when I go,

Do not cry for me too much"

This Hurts

This hurt is so immense,
I cannot imagine going through it again,
I know that Death is inevitable.
It is just a matter of when.

I cannot imagine a world,
Without the people that I love and care for,
I hope and pray for them to be safe,
And stay with me healthy and happy, for so much
longer.

I sat thinking the other day,
About a world without my parents,
And that is something I never ever,
Ever, want to experience.

But at the same time, I recognize,
With solemn certainty,
That it's better for them to go first,
So they never have to mourn for me.

Coping with the aftermath of loss
And the disillusion of our control,
I will understand but resent Death
If he returns for my beloveds before me.

Sharif's Villanelle

You were always older, wiser and more mature
Now I'm two years older and
I don't know anything anymore

Around and within, are massacres and wars
You would've been vocal about stolen lands
You were always older, wiser and more mature

A young boy to a diligent man, born in Lahore
And now... where are you and what of our plans?
I don't know anything anymore

Our kinship engraved with axiomatic poetry and folklore
Now I sit with my denial of our unexpected paths
You were always older, wiser and more mature

Now all I can do is cry in sujood and pray for
The friend who I thought I could understand
I don't know anything anymore

You had all these dreams and wishes, you swore
And so ... I missed all the red flags
You were always older, wiser and more mature
I don't know anything anymore

I miss you,
I see you in everything you used to do,
And all the memories we share.

I miss you,
I see you in the flora you took care of,
And all the fruit your trees now bear.

I miss you,
I see your life through scattered photos,
And wonder how many were taken that I haven't yet
seen.

I miss you,
I look for you in your books I borrowed,
Well... stole, from your library

I miss you,
I miss the creek of your rocker,
And seeing you comfortable in your seat.

I miss you,
I miss hearing you tell me you love me,
And I miss being able to hug you.

I miss you,
And your soulful, brightening laugh that came from the
heart,
I miss our little talks, where we filled each other in on
the happenings of when we were apart.

I miss you,
And I wish I could see you now,
But I know I have to wait.

I miss you,
But I know that one day,
We'll see each other again.

I miss you,
And your sage wisdom as a mentor,
And all the advice you won't be able to impart
anymore.

I miss you,
And I love you,
Now, always and forevermore.

"I miss you,

I look for you in your books..."

Part IV
Always &
Forever

Ephemeral

How strange and beautiful it is
That our lives are so rich with wonder and stardust
Short and fleeting as it may seem,
When compared to our Universe's vast, ethereal
grandeur

What lies before, and what lies after,
What we know, and we have yet to learn,
What we have seen, and what we yearn to see,
What we believe, and what we dream.

In the infinitude of Time and Space,
The evanescence of our lives, in itself,
Is intricately woven into the Cosmos,
Etched in the moon's craters and colours of the Earth.

We were here, and we were beautiful and disastrous,
And we tried, and we didn't always try hard enough.
Our world will taste of our memory long after we are
gone,
Even if we weren't here for that long.

For Your Loss

I'm sorry,
Though I know these words are both
Heavy in my sincerity
And empty in its helplessness.

I'm sorry,
That I cannot bring them back,
No matter how my heart yearns to,
That I could not save them for you.

I'm sorry,
That I steal away your tears and agony,
I would bury it so deep you would be cursed to forever
be happy,
But I know that mourning is a necessity.

I'm sorry,
That I cannot fill in the crevices
Of all the funeral flowers and bereavement cards
With what you wish to know and hear, all the answers.

I'm sorry,
There is no conceivable way to make it better
There is no going back to the Before,
Your life has changed forever.

I'm sorry,
For your loss,
And this love now as sombre, seizing grief,

But I hope you snuggle with the fond, happy memories
of them,
And never forget the good times of how it used to be.

I'm sorry,
That it's hard and there's nothing I can do to make it
better,
But this pain you feel, is just love that will last
forevermore.

"But this pain you feel, is just love that will last
forevermore."

This Grief Is Ours

I see my grief amplified in your eyes,
And it breaks my heart for the millionth time.
There is nothing I can do, to make this easier
So that you'll be alright.
There are no words I can share,
To take away any of your grief.

Every time I see your heart break,
I resent my helplessness and pray for your healing,
But I know nothing can change
This way we are feeling.

Every time I see your tears pool
And every time I hear your cries,
I just wish I could put everything back together,
The way it was, by holding you tight.

I love you so much, and I feel your grief,
I know you are sad and hallow, just like me.
I know you miss them, just like I do.
I hope you know that out there, beyond the Heavens,
They are looking on, and love you too.

"There are no words I can share,

To take away any of your grief."

Patience

A grieving heart is one of sorrow,
Longing for an unrecognizable love
Trying to put haphazard pieces of her life together,
But they don't fit, and everything is different now.

Finally, when she makes progress,
And almost sees the bigger picture,
She finds a missing hole, left by Fate,
Promised in every scripture of an ending and a
beginning.

Listening illuminates what she needs to find peace,
To understand the gravity and agony of grief.
You must understand the hollowness of her accepting
that empty space,
That can *never* be replaced.

The mourning heart may not know what to do,
Either clinging to find out what went wrong,
Or flinging what was built thus far as anger brews
Or just taking a walk and trying to be strong.

Whatever the heart needs to be okay,
In this moment of utter heartache and dismay
Please be patient with the grieving hearts,
For they are just doing what they must, to not break
apart.

"Please be patient with the grieving hearts,

For they are just doing what they must, to not break apart."

Darling, I'll Pray For You

In every prayer I have prayed,
Since you have been gone,
I pray for you,
For your peace and God's mercy on your soul.

I pray for your legacy to live on
In those who remain behind,
And your goodness to infect
All the ones who basked in your light.

I pray for any of your sins,
Few, small and all, to be wholly forgiven,
And any you may have hurt, to remember your love,
And think of you fondly from now on.

I pray for you to be comfortable wherever you are,
And for God to embrace you in his loving arms.
I pray for your ascension to the Highest of the Heavens,
I pray to have even an ounce of your goodness.

I pray that your dreams for us become a reality,
I pray that somehow, some way, you can see them
come true,
I pray that you know we will always love you,
And I know while you wait, you love me too.

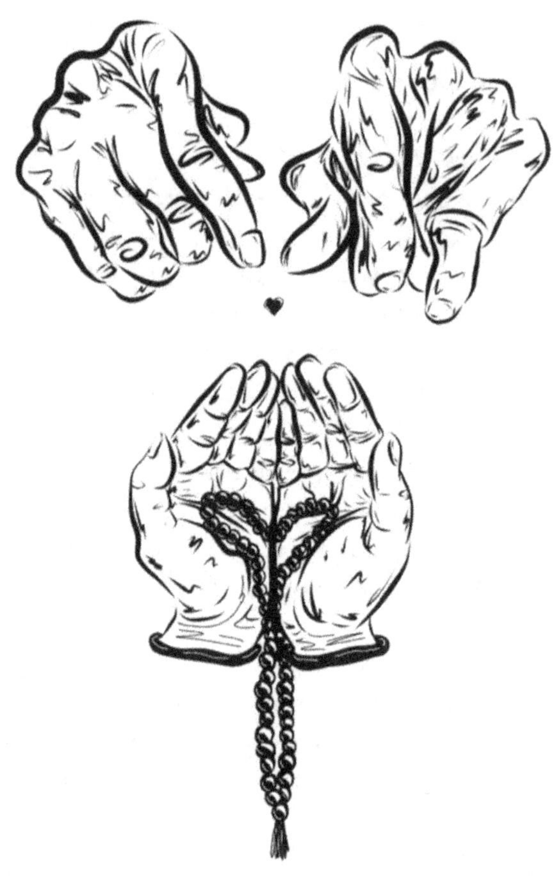

4

4 This drawing was inspired by a photo taken by my cousin Raisa of my Grandma Afrose's hands. Mama was afflicted with rheumatoid arthritis which caused severe warping of her hands in her winter years. But those same hands prayed every day. And when I was younger, her hands combed my hair, and held my own as we went off on adventures. This art piece depicts the love that lasts long after those we love are gone, through our prayers and remembrance of them.

Nose

I do my best to keep my nose
Out of other people's business,
Focus on my own trials and troubles,
And only listen to what I need to.

She said she knows we were related,
Because of our distinguishable Beharry nose,
The same one kids used to joke was too big,
But now we proudly scrunch when we see our family.

And in those last few days, knowing what was coming,
I was so nosey, asking you everything I could
About everything I could think of
To commit to memory of all the things I would know.

There are things I may never know,
And I don't know how to reconcile that yet,
But I know I'll carry your nose with me everywhere,
Every deep breath, full of love and gratitude
for the time I had with you.

Heavenly Birthday

Today would have been your birthday
We would have celebrated with a delicious cake,
Cleaned and decorated the house
Brought balloons and flowers and all the works

We would have searched far and wide for the perfect
gift
Knowing you'd love anything we could ever bring
But we'd want it to be perfect, and just for you
Because we love you so much and we know you love
us too

We would have pulled the family into the same room
And prayed together for you to be healthy, safe and
okay
And then taken individual pics with you and your cake
And laughed and sang and danced the night away

Today is the day you were brought into this world
To leave a lasting impression on all those who knew you
Like a gorgeous flower, your life beautifully bloomed,
petals unfurled,
And now you have returned to God and to the earth,

I hope you know we think of you today, on your
heavenly birthday
And continue to pray for you
As we do and will continue to, always.

Promise Me, Please?

"Please don't go
Before your time,"
Is all I can think to say,

"Think of your future,
And all that could be,
If you just... choose to stay.

I know I may not know it,
How you feel, and how you have been hurt.
But I will do all I can,
To show you, just how much your life is worth.

I don't have all the right words,
I quite possibly never will,
But I hope you hear the haphazard ones that I do have,
And decide to stay, still.

I won't tell you to think of others,
But I will remind you that you are loved.
I won't ask you to live for anyone else,
But I will implore you to search for a purpose.

Live for you,
Not for anyone else.
If you don't have dreams,
Find, build, and live them.
Meet people and make friends,
Fill your days with the liquor of love,
And the high of unadulterated happiness.

When anyone asks you who saved you,
Tell them YOU did,
Tell them you crawled out of that claustrophobic cocoon
yourself and lived.
Live each day to the fullest.
Live each day knowing you may never know when it's
your last.

No matter your past,
Breathe in each moment, knowing it can be stolen in a
moment's notice,
And when you are struggling,
Remember you are not alone, you are loved,
Everything will be fine,
And promise yourself, to please do not go,
Before it is your time"

The Point

What is the point of anything?
Why do we learn and grow and work?
If it is inevitable, that we just return to the earth?
Why do we buy houses, new cars and clothes?
When we all know where we're going,
From the time we have been birthed.
Why do we lose ourselves in novels and movies,
And exercising and consuming healthy foods?
When dying is something that nothing can change,
No matter what we do.

There is no wasted time,
For every precious memory holds a stolen moment,
Paid by joyful smiles or growing lessons.
To live is to experience life in its fullest of ways,
By doing what you love, with whom you love
With our limited time in this place.

Non dolet, Paete!

Our plans weren't forged in stone,
But now they'll be etched into our history,
Forever intombed in my diary, for none to see
My voice you can never again hear, and the books you
will never read.

Your death is alive in my mind,
A hollow paradox, heavy in its burdening albatross,
Flying around my head, lost in the clouds searching for
you in the Heavens,
Knowing long since that I had shattered, long having
fallen,
Lying in a cataclysmic crater caused by the terminal
choice you've taken

On the crossroads of where our trains have now
departed in separate ways,
I wonder if one day I will ever again see your face,
The whistle echoes in my mind when I think of your last
wave good-bye,
And how the birds likely flew South in anticipation of
my impending iciness.

Those who don't understand how hearts can intertwine
over seas and across borders,
Will resign to viewing my grief as strange and piteous.
But those who never received the answers to questions
no one can answer,
Will be the only ones who could ever understand a story
unfinished...

A moment of vulnerability, a gesture to share one's
rarely shared words,
An abundance of time to think of its unfaltering lack
thereof for another,
And the delivery of The News of the loss of my life,
And the unwritten and withheld messages that will
forever haunt my mind.

Paete, non dolet!
Is what you assumed I would say,
But all that consumes me is pain
That I would endure forevermore if it meant you could
stay.

For Those I Love

Your love strengthens me when I am falling;
It pulls me back up and together.
You give me purpose and direction,
Even when I think I would never see a light again

Your love enriches my soul
With the sweet dew of your words and shared
sustenance,
You give me something to look forward and up to,
I know you'll always be there when I need you.

You give me space when I need it,
You nourish my life with your constant light,
You give me room to grow, while always being there for
support,
It's like you just always know, how to help, how to
ensure I feel loved.

You give me a reason to live,
You remind me why I must keep on going and growing,
You refine, deepen and ameliorate my finite time here,
With your showers of fond memories for me to cherish,
And I will hold these close to my heart and soul,
As we flourish, and till the grave and beyond when we
inevitably must perish.

"You give me purpose and direction,

Even when I think I would never see
a light again"

Remember me

I know it's never easy for anybody,
But it was inevitably difficult to write your eulogy.
I thought of how you would want to be remembered,
And what others would want to know and hear.
I considered all the stories you would tell us,
And in your winter days, the ones you chose to share.
I poured each anecdote into words that strung together,
Into a tribute, I was proud to write but didn't know if I
could read.
I read it, in front of a mirror,
And found myself struggling to breathe.
I practised it a few times, until the words
Were just air escaping my mouth in different ways,
Until I shared it with our family, on your funeral day.

Death makes us think about the living,
And how we choose to lead our own lives in the
present.
I think about how I would want to be remembered,
And as a woman of many hats, I am unsure of how I
would be represented.

A story of sacrifice is my parents' legacy,
Cut my noble mother and you would find love before
she could ever bleed.
My knight of a father would ride to save anyone in
need.
Their creed was being the change they wished to see.

Would you remember me as kind,

For I tried
My very best, to give my heart and soul
To all who wanted to pack a piece of it, to go?

Would you remember me as a mastermind,
In the ways I traded time
For misery and resume lines,
So that I could have a good life.

Would you remember me as a poet,
For the words I ripped out of my lowest
Self to share with people who would skim for a few
And place my broken heart back on the shelf?

Would you remember me as an artist,
Who tried her hardest to keep her self-promise
Of creating beautiful, unique works,
In a world full of diverse master-pieces?

Would I be remembered as someone who loved?
Whose wholehearted love stained her blood,
Who dotted... and crossed her every word,
A love story to be forever, in time, preserved?

Would you remember every aspect of me,
From my silliest schemes to make you laugh with me,
To all of my dutiful stories and hobbies,
And to my Machiavellian tendencies to make you love
me?

When it is inevitably my time to go,

Whether you think of me fondly, or whether you don't,
My soul shall live on in the writing I leave behind,
For another sad, lonely girl in a Literature class to find.

"*A story of sacrifice is my parents'*
legacy,

Cut my noble mother and you
would find love before she could
ever bleed.

My knight of a father would ride to
save anyone in need."

Our Dreams

Sometimes in my dreams,
You come to visit me.
I dream of you strong and happy,
And I think, it helps me to heal.
It reminds me that you are both out there in the
heavens,
But also, in my memories and my heart, here with me.
I have your gifted trinkets and presents,
And relish in the ones I could never give away.
In my slumber, you speak with me softly,
And eventually sing me awake.
In my dreams, you attend my future wedding,
As a braided luck sewn into my heart,
And when you eventually part ways again,
You take with you, new stories for your journey back.
You bring meaning and joy to the sleep
That I once took for granted as a child,
And I hope in all my dreams,
You will be proud of me
For how much I continue to work and try hard.

Grief Holds Us Together[5]

The first time Death passed through my life
I was far too young to comprehend what it meant,
I thought He would just deliver a ticket to be collected
later,
So travellers could give hugs, and "goodbye" for closure.
Photos and stories would flood social media,
As they left for their permanent destination.

Death took the girl who sat beside me in class when I
was 6 years old.
I remember thinking I could attend the funeral
Thinking she'd just gotten a ticket to the afterlife,
And would be around so I could give her a hug,
"goodbye."
My mum sat me down to console me,
"She's in a better place," mommy promised.

Years later, Death would be but a pumpkin-vine relative,
Passing by every now and then,
Unswayed by age, gender, race, wealth or environment,
Taking my teachers, family members and even a friend.
As He went with them, the air would be humid and
cold,
We would clutch one another,
Indelible tears and old sadness breathed between us.

---

[5] This poem was originally written for the Bereaved Families
of Ontario for the Butterflies of Hope event in 2022, and since
then it has evolved as Grief passed through my ever-changing
life

In high school, I would face two great traumas,
The first was losing my Arabic teacher Aunty Finah
The kindest, old lady who taught me to read the Qur'an
I would go on to write many poems about her.
But the hardest was a young girl who had a seizure
Two other prefects and I tried our very best
One holding her feet, the other her head,
While I held her hands and promised she would be okay
To wandering eyes that I would never see again after
that day
A night of worrying and a day of rumours would slip by
Before all we would see, were pictures from her friends
online
And the cries of teens,
Wanting to ask her what she wanted for Christmas
Angels and Earthlings.
I suppose she's their angel now.
I don't know how if their teacher made them repick
names,
I never had the strength to visit that class again.

When Death returned for Mama Afrose,
She welcomed Him as an old friend,
Calmly following him into the unknown,
While around her, we all prayed and wept and wept and
wept.
Death left behind Grief, who I'd only been acquainted
with in passing.
And she's like a 'harden' child - worse yet, like an
ignorant adult,
A sickness, an exhaustion, an "I just passing through"

But 40 Days have long passed and she still not looking
doesn't appear to be leaving
And no one really knows what to do with her.

"Time heals all wounds" and "It gets better" and all
those cliches
To so many condolence bouquets of flowers
That you forget you're supposed to be breathing
oxygen, not sorrow.
And people will give you lectures and books on how life
goes on,
But days feel cruel without the ones we love.
We see them in every little trinket their memory holds
on to
All the things we never got to say,
Every page they ever wrote on lost, somewhere in the
world
Every word they never wrote down, full of meaning and
purpose
Every drawing we could pin on fridges and frame on
walls,
Every unforgettable unspoken promise of love.

But this is not the end,
Our loved ones are not gone forever,
They live on, through us, in our words, in our actions, in
our reminiscence.
We may not see them right now,
But their memory is etched into the photos we've saved,
Into the places, they have grown up in or visited,
Their laughter may be replayed in videos

And their art and letters may be saved in books,
They are not gone,
Their impression is one with the world.

That said, sometimes these things we hold on to,
Don't make it any easier
With the infinite unknown of what is after life.
Will our paths cross again?
Will they be waiting for us, to hold our hands and walk
us over?
Will we see them again, and will we hold each other
and laugh like before?
Are they watching over us right now, praying for us to
be okay,
Sometimes visiting in dreams, to let us know they're not
far away?

Grief is heavy; it weighs down on our souls like an
ancient curse
Happiness is light, like a helium balloon, easily flown
away
But as soon as it's gone,
The heftiness of grief, remembrance and nostalgia, is
what remains.

Sometimes it may be an empty bed,
The hollowness of what would have been a hug on
sleepless nights,
Sometimes it may be old shirts you can't get rid of
The smell, you wish you could bottle up and never
forget and save forever

Weddings and funerals bring the people we love
together
Our grief, our love for them, holds us together
Our hearts have been a warm home for them to stay a
while,
We share our memories of how we loved them and
smile

We must cherish their lives,
Mark the good they have done,
Honour the light they've brought to the dark world,
Acknowledge the lives they've impacted
All the people they made smile

Like us, like you,
They would want us to live on, while we can

We spend our finite time missing them
Sometimes forgetting the other people we love,
So many lives left to touch.
There are so many things we wish we could say
To our loved ones who have passed on;

In the wake of death, we shouldn't forget the people
around us today
Helping us to hold on
To some semblance of a new normalcy
Of heavy sorrow and empty hollowness.
Embrace the people who support you,

Hug them tight, and tell them how you feel while you
can,
Tell them that you love them,
For Time is unforgiving to those who never got to
profess.

Grief is a young child whose nickname is Love,
Together we'll hold her hand tightly
To cross the intersection of tomorrow and forever
Making sure she isn't taken away by a stranger
Sometimes she'll go to the park,
Sometimes she'll visit friends,
Sometimes you'll be so lost in the moment
That - for just a second - you forget she's there,
And she'll return, and hold your hand with a smile,
And you'll hug her to sleep, and the pain will subside for
a while,
And she'll stay with you to remind you of love,
All the people around you who shower you with it,
And all the people you have loved and are gone now,
And how even though time is limited,
Love is infinite.

The Best of Planners

God is the Best of Planners,
You lived a beautiful life,
And you were proud of the life you lived.
What favours of our Lord can we then deny?

God is the Best of Planners,
And He said that it was time,
He was ready for you to come home,
And leave us here, leave us behind.

God is the Best of Planners,
This kind of pain that will never go away,
Is here for a reason, to help me grow,
To forge strength and faith.

God is the Best of Planners,
I believe we will meet again,
On the crossroads to Heaven,
Where we will spend eternity, God-willing.

"What favours of our Lord can we
then deny?"

Still Here

For as long as you are still here,
I will keep you close and near.
You whisper almost-lies and sweet nothings like "I'm here
my dear"
As you slip away, and I fall into despair.

For as long as I am still here,
I will remind you that there is nothing to fear,
That I love you with my whole heart bared,
And I will leave behind for you all its shares.

For as long as I am still here,
I will lovingly watch over you as you carefully steer
Into a new life without me there.
You won't know but I will always be in your heart,
right here.

Part V
Before You Go

Loss is a pain that we must all face at some point in our lives. It's difficult and hard, and it affects everyone in different ways.

We all have different coping mechanisms and while not all are positive ones — we should make space for people to mourn in their own way, while offering our support and love in whichever ways we can.

Sometimes the people we love don't know how they need to cope either. Let them process their grief, and just be there for them. Ensure, if you are able to, that they know you are there for them — either to listen, lend a helping hand, distracting them to think of something else, or giving them company or space, whatever they need.

It is a strange type of despair to watch someone you love in pain, and not be able to do anything about it. It's hard to come to terms with the fact that sometimes, we can just be helpless. What we must understand is that we can only control what we can... so we do what we can. And everything else, we just have to deal with when it arises.

I will not tell you to be strong or try to be okay. Those things come with time. Remember to be patient with yourself. Keep some of the abundant strength and love that you have for others, for yourself.

If you ever need someone to talk to, know that there's someone out there who loves you and will be there to listen.

While it may seem like there is only darkness right now...

Soon the darkness too shall slip away,

And the sun's glorious light will come out again.

All we didn't know
Is now lost to us,
But found by ancestors forevermore.

All that we were not prepared for,
But how could anyone accept
That someone is soon to be gone?

In those last few days,
We asked questions and took notes,
Etched your final words into our hearts and soul.

Fortunate to have the chance to barter
Answers for infinite love,
As some don't even get a good-bye,
Much less a hug.

Grasp every moment,
Not a second too late,
Ask what you wish to,
Before you can never again.

A fond memory I will always cherish with ____________
is:

My favourite things about ________________________
will always be:

I will always remember ________________________________ as:

If I could say one more thing to _______________,
it would be:

I want to be remembered as:

If I had one more day, I would:

106

One secret I never told anyone, that I was prepared to take to the grave is:

Will

Will you be okay?

What Will I leave behind?

Later on Will I even be remembered?

What precious memories Will come to mind when you think of me?

And if so, how Will I be remembered?

After I am long gone, Will I still have a place in your heart?

When you think of me, how Will you feel?

Some of my favourite things in life were:

This is not legally binding, but if I could bequeath it to someone, it would be to:

Sketch or place a photo of someone you love here. It can be someone who has passed on, or someone you hold dearly and would miss them if they were gone.

The love in your heart for this person is reflected by someone who loves you as well. You are not alone. You will never be alone. There will always be someone out there who appreciates that you are here.

Notes